# The Ultimate Ceviche Chef

## The Art Of Central American Cuisine

by Ann Sullivan

Published in USA by:

Ann Sullivan
217 N. Seacrest Blvd #9
Boynton Beach
FL 33425

© Copyright 2016

ISBN-13: 978-1540345783
ISBN-10: 1540345785

# Table of Contents

# Ceviche Supreme

## Ingredients

1 lb. seafood, sushi grade (shrimp, scallops, whitefish)
1 1/2 cups fresh lime juice
2 pickled jalapeno peppers, minced
1 onion, chopped
1 tomato, skinned, cubed
6 tbsps. olive oil
2 tbsps. white wine vinegar
1/4 tsp. oregano
1/2 tsp. fresh pepper, ground
1/2 tsp. salt
12 lime wedges

## Directions

Clean and rinse fish. Dry fish with clean cloth. Remove skin and bones. Shred skin and bones.
If needed, shell and devein all seafood. Place all seafood in casserole dish. Cover seafood in lime juice. Refrigerate dish for 2 hours. After 2 hours stir contents and refrigerate for another 2 hours.
Remove dish from refrigerator, and drain lime juice.
Blend jalapenos, onion, oil, tomato, vinegar, salt, pepper, and oregano in a bowl. Pour tomato mixture into dish completely coating fish mixture. Refrigerate for 3 hours, then remove. Bring to room temperature for 15 minutes. Garnish with lime wedges. Option: Add lemon juice instead of lime juice.

# Ceviche

## Ingredients

1 lb. fresh tuna or orange roughie or red snapper (any firm-fleshed whitefish)
3 lemons, juice of
3 limes, juice of
1 garlic clove, minced
1 onion, minced
1 jalapeno or poblano pepper, chopped fine
2 tbsps. cilantro, finely chopped
2 tbsps. parsley
Salt
1 avocado, sliced (optional)

## Directions

Soak fish in salt water for 10 minutes. Dry fish with a paper towel. Cut fish into cubes. Put cubes into a shallow dish. Place onions atop fish. Place all remaining ingredients atop fish. Refrigerate at least 4 hours. Garnish with avocado. Serve chilled.

# Mexican Ceviche

## Ingredients

1 lb. halibut fillet, sea bass fillet, or red snapper fillet (or use a mixture of fish and shrimp)
5-6 limes (enough juice to cover fish)
1 cup fresh tomato, diced
1 green pepper, sweet, chopped
4 tbsps. parsley or cilantro, chopped
1/4 tsp. salt
1/4 tsp. pepper
1/2 tsp. oregano
2 jalapeno peppers, chopped (or more to suit your taste)
2 tbsps. white vinegar
1 medium onion, finely chopped
2 tbsps. fresh cilantro, chopped
1 dash Tabasco sauce
Lettuce leaf (to line serving bowls)
Avocado (optional)
Black olives, sliced (for garnish) (optional)

## Directions

Cut fish into ½" squares, and place squares in a casserole dish. [If using shrimp, use cleaned shrimp.] Add lime juice to dish and refrigerate overnight. Stir often across the night to ensure proper marinating. In the morning, remove most of the lime juice leaving fish moist. Place all remaining ingredients except lettuce, avocado, and olive in dish.

**Note:** Do last step a few hours before serving and then refrigerate. Line individual serving bowls with lettuce leaves. Thoroughly mix and arrange in the individual serving bowls. Garnish with sliced avocado and sliced black olives.

# Radish Ceviche

## Ingredients

Radish
Lime Juice

## Directions

Creatively slice radishes into interesting shapes. Soak radishes in lime juice for 24 hours.

# Simply Ceviche

## Ingredients

1/4 lb. fresh bay scallop, cut into quarters
3 limes, juice of
1 tbsp. cilantro, minced
2 tbsps. red onions, chopped
2 tsps. fresh basil, chopped
2 green onions, chopped
1/2 green bell pepper, diced
1/2 red bell pepper, diced
1/2 yellow bell pepper, diced
1 (8 oz.) can stewed tomatoes
1 pinch black pepper

## Directions

Place scallops in a large bowl. Marinate scallops in lime juice. Cover bowl and place it in the refrigerator overnight. Remove lime juice leaving scallops moist. Add remaining ingredients. Thoroughly blend mixture. Marinate for 2 1/2 hours in refrigerator. Serve chilled with crackers.

# Lime Ceviche

## Ingredients

1/4 cup lime juice, freshly squeezed
1 jalapeno pepper, seeded and diced
1 tsp. fresh ginger, grated
1 tbsp. extra-virgin olive oil
1 lb. shrimp or firm sea bass or halibut, skins removed
and cut into ½" cubes
3 scallions, white and light-green parts only, thinly sliced
on the bias
1 cucumber, cut into matchsticks
1/4 cup fresh mint leaves
1/4 cup fresh cilantro leaves
1 avocado, peeled, pitted, and cut into ½" cubes
(optional)
Salt and freshly ground black pepper

## Directions

Combine juice, jalapeño, ginger, and oil in a mixing bowl.
Add shrimp or fish to the mixture. Thoroughly blend all
contents. Cover bowl with plastic. Chill in refrigerator,
occasionally stirring, until flesh is opaque. Note: This
process should take at least 1 hour. Add all remaining
ingredients and thoroughly mix. Season with salt and
pepper as needed. Blend well and serve.

# Argentine Ceviche

## Ingredients

1 lb. sea scallops or bay scallop, rinsed (if using sea scallops, cut into bite-size pieces)
8 limes, juice of
1 1/4 cups onions, chopped
1/2 cup Spanish olives, pits removed and sliced into quarters
2 tbsps. olive brine, from jar
3 tomatoes, peeled and chopped, with juice reserved
1 (14 oz.) bottle Heinz hot catsup (or 1 3/4 cups plain catsup mixed with 1 tbsp. dried red pepper flakes)
1 tbsp. crumbled dried oregano

## Directions

Place scallops in a glass or ceramic bowl. Coat scallops with lime juice. Place lid on bowl and refrigerate for 3 hours. Combine all remaining ingredients in a separate bowl, blend them well. Cover the sauce, and store it at room temperature. When scallops are marinated, remove the lime juice. Rinse scallops using cold running water. Dry scallops with paper towels. Combine scallops with sauce and mix well. Cover bowl and refrigerate overnight until ready to serve.

# Shrimp Ceviche

## Ingredients

3 stalks celery, diced
3 bell peppers, diced (Red, Yellow, Green)
1 lb. frozen shrimp (shelled, diced)
1 bunch cilantro (remove stems, wash and chop)
4 limes, juice of
1/2 cup zesty Italian salad dressing
Salt
2 dashes cayenne pepper, to taste

## Directions

Thoroughly blend all ingredients in a mixing bowl. Refrigerate bowl for at least 1 hour. Serve with tortilla chips.

# Scallop Ceviche

## Ingredients

16 scallops gutted and clean
1 tsp. fresh lemon rind, finely grated
1 chile pepper, seeded and finely chopped
60 ml lemon juice
2 garlic cloves, finely chopped
1 tbsp. coriander, finely chopped
1 tbsp. olive oil

## Directions

Place all ingredients in a glass bowl. Add scallops and mix well. Seal bowl airtight with plastic wrap. Set bowl in the refrigerator for 2 hours. Note: The scallops will be "cooked" by the juice when flesh turns white. Place scallops on small plates. Ladle a small amount of lemon-juice marinade onto each scallop. Garnish dish with a few coriander leaves. Serve the scallops cold.

# Ceviche Tacos

## Ingredients

3-4 limes
1 cup tomato, chopped and seeded
1 cup avocado, peeled and diced
1/2 cup cilantro, chopped
3/4 tsp. salt
1/4 tsp. pepper
3 garlic cloves, minced
1 lb. medium shrimp, peeled and cooked
Corn tortilla

## Directions

Grate lime rinds making 1 tbsp. of rind. Juice limes making 1/4 cup of juice. Place rind and juice in a glass bowl. Add tomato, avocado, cilantro, salt, pepper, garlic and shrimp to bowl.

Option: Add chopped onions and fresh jalapenos to bowl as well. Blend well to create a homogenous mixture. Place a lid on bowl and chill for 15 minutes in refrigerator. Occasionally stir contents during refrigeration. Heat tortillas in oven or warm them in microwave. Place half a cup of shrimp mixture on center of tortilla; fold and eat.

Option: Instead of tortillas, try crackers, hard taco shells, or tortilla chips.

# Tahitian Ceviche

## Ingredients

1 lb. fresh Ahi (fresh tuna will suffice)
1/2 quart lightly salt water (I like sea salt for this)
1 tsp. salt
1 cup lime juice (must be fresh)
1 cup unsweetened coconut milk
1 tomato, finely chopped
1 small onion, finely chopped
1 red bell pepper, seeded and finely chopped
1 dash Tabasco sauce
Salt

## Directions

Across grain, cut fish into small pieces. Place pieces in a pan with salt water. Let sit for 30 minutes. Remove liquid from pan. Place lime juice and salt in pan. Work marinating solution into fish pieces. Let mixture marinate for 5 minutes. When fish becomes white, add all remaining ingredients. Thoroughly mix, let sit for at least 60 minutes.

# Mushroom Ceviche

## Ingredients

1 lb. fresh mushrooms, sliced
1 cup red onion, chopped
2 cups tomatoes, diced
1 cup cilantro, chopped
1 Habanero pepper, chopped
1/4 cup olive oil
Salt and pepper
2 to 3 limes, juice of

## Directions

Soften mushrooms by steaming them. Let mushrooms cool. Place all remaining ingredients in a bowl. Refrigerate and serve with tostadas or crackers.

# Shrimp Ceviche

## Ingredients

3 limes (squeezed)
2 tbsps. garlic (chopped)
1/4 tsp. pepper (ground)
1/4 tsp. salt
1 lb. frozen shrimp, uncooked, peeled
1/2 medium red onion, thinly sliced
1 jalapeno, seeded and chopped
1/4 cup Italian parsley or cilantro, chopped

## Directions

Thaw shrimp by placing them in a bowl filled with cold water. Place bowl in the sink. Allow water from faucet to drip into bowl until overflowing. Fill medium pan with water. Boil over high heat. When thawed, put shrimp in a bowl filled with hot water. Let sit for a few minutes until shrimp pink and not translucent. Remove water from pan. Halve shrimp lengthwise [from head to tail]. Let cut shrimp completely cool. Combine lime juice, garlic, salt and pepper in a blender. Puree mixture until thoroughly combined, and place in a bowl. Add shrimp, onion, jalapeno, and parsley [or cilantro] to puree. Add lime mixture to bowl. Let sit for at least 30 minutes.

# Shrimp Ceviche

## Ingredients

2-3 lbs. shrimp, peeled and deveined
2 large tomatoes, diced
1 red onion, diced
1 bunch cilantro, diced
1 Serrano pepper or jalapeno, diced
8 limes, squeezed
8 lemons, squeezed
2 oranges, squeezed (preferably sour oranges)
2 large avocados, diced
2 large cucumbers, peeled and diced

## Directions

To blanch shrimp, first place them into boiling water for 5 minutes. Then plunge them into freezing water. When cooled, drain water. Create 1-inch pieces of shrimp by cutting them with a knife. Place these pieces in a glass bowl. Pour citrus juice into the bowl. Let shrimp marinate for 2 hours. Place onion, tomatoes, chilies and cilantro in the bowl. Let mixture marinate for an additional 2 hours. Place avocados and cucumbers atop the mixture.

# Shrimp Ceviche

## Ingredients

2 medium cucumbers
1 large red bell pepper
1 large orange bell pepper
1 large yellow bell pepper
1 medium poblano chile or Serrano chile pepper
1/2 large red onion
1 bunch fresh cilantro
1 cup lime juice (fresh preferred, bottled okay)
1 1/4 lbs. raw shrimp, butterflied and deveined (21-30 count)

## Directions

Remove ends from cucumbers, and cut into four lengthwise strips. Further cut these strips creating several ¼" pieces, and remove seeds. Put cucumbers in a bowl with lid. Process bell peppers in a similar manner and put in the bowl. Slice onion in half, peel it, and place the flat side down on a cutting board. Cut off the top and bottom, then create small strips and put in the bowl. Dice the chile pepper, remove seeds and put in the bowl. Zest limes and put zest in the bowl. While bowl mixture marinates, peel, devein, and butterfly the raw shrimp. Thoroughly rinse shrimp and place in a bag. Add two thirds of the lime juice to the bag.

[Option: Mix lime and lemon juice.] Mince cilantro,

saving a few intact leaves to use later as a garnish. Put chopped cilantro in the bowl and cover bowl. Vigorously shake bowl to completely mix ingredients. Open bowl and pour in the remaining lime juice. Reseal bowl and refrigerate for several hours. Flip bag and shake bowl regularly during marinating process. Combine contents of bag and bowl. Serve shrimp whole or chop into large pieces. Garnish with the leftover cilantro leaves. Serve with tortilla chips.

**Option:** Serve with sliced and toasted baguette bread.

# Shrimp Ceviche

## Ingredients

1 lb. medium-small shrimp, peeled and deveined
2 tbsps. salt
3/4 cup lime juice (juice from 4-6 limes)
3/4 cup lemon juice (juice from 2-3 lemons)
1 cup red onion, finely chopped
1 Serrano chili, ribs and seeds removed, minced
1 cup cilantro, chopped
1 small cucumber, peeled diced into ½" pieces
1 avocado, peeled, seed removed, cut into ½" chunks
4 small lettuce leaves
Corn tortilla or tortilla chips

## Directions

Bring a pan of salt water to a boil. Add shrimp for 1-2 minutes.

[Note: Don't overcook as it'll make shrimp rubbery.] Remove shrimp, place in a bowl of freezing water to stop the cooking process. Drain the bow leaving shrimp moist. Halve shrimp, or cut into inch-long pieces. Put shrimp in a glass or ceramic bowl. Pour the citrus juice into the bowl. Cover bowl and refrigerate contents for 30 minutes. Add the chopped red onion and Serrano chile. Stir and place in refrigerator for an additional 30 minutes. Add the cilantro, cucumber, and avocado immediately before serving. Use the lettuce leaves as a garnish. Serve wrapped in tortillas or with chips.

# Ceviche Salad

## Ingredients

1 cup cooked shrimp, peeled and deveined
1 cucumber, peeled and diced
1 tomato, diced
1/2 avocado, diced
1/4 cup prepared mango salsa
1/2 lime, juice of,
Salt and pepper

## Directions

Place all ingredients in a glass or ceramic bowl.
Thoroughly mix contents. Place bowl in refrigerator.
Serve this Ceviche salad with tortilla chips.

# Tuna Ceviche

## Ingredients

2 cups V8 vegetable juice
1 large onion, chopped
3 medium tomatoes, chopped
1 lemon, juice of
1/2 tsp. lemon zest, fresh
2 (7 oz.) cans albacore tuna, drained, flaked
1 cup green olive, chopped
1/4 tsp. oregano, scant, powdered
1/4 tsp. Tabasco sauce

## Directions

Add juice, onion, tomatoes, oregano and sauce to a glass or ceramic bowl. Refrigerate bowl until contents are chilled. Sprinkle lemon juice onto tuna. Let stand for 30 minutes. Place tuna into tomato mixture and add olives. Refrigerate again. When chilled, pour into bowls. When serving, place an ice cube in each bowl and sprinkle with zest.

# Ceviche and Shrimp Ceviche

## Ingredients

7 oz. octopus, cooked
Shrimp, tails blanched
7 oz. scallops
1 red onion, sliced very fine
1/2 red Aji limo chile, minced
1/2 yellow Aji limo chile, minced
16 key limes, juice of
Salt
2 sweet potatoes, boiled
1 large fresh ear corn on the cob, cooked and cut into rounds

## Directions

If using adult octopus, cut it into small pieces.

[Note: If using baby octopus, leave it uncut.] For squid, cut it into small rings. Combine seafood and onion in large bowl. Thoroughly wash and completely drain. Add salt and chilies to mixture. Place mixture in lime juice, and vigorously shake. Place a few ice cubes into mixture and re-shake. Remove ice before it melts. Place on bed of lettuce, sweet potatoes and boiled corn rounds.

# Ceviche Corvina

## Ingredients

1 3/4 lbs. sea bass or flounder fillets
1 red onion, very finely sliced
1/2 red Aji limo chile, chopped very fine
1/2 yellow Aji limo Chile, chopped very fine
16 key limes, juice of
Salt
1 ear corn on the cob, boiled and cut into rounds
Boiled sweet potato
Lettuce leaf

## Directions

Cut fish into small pieces. Mix with onion in large bowl.
Wash onion and fish. Remove excess liquid. Season with
salt and chilies. Place fish in lime juice, and vigorously
shake. Add ice cubes, and mix well. Remove cubes before
they melt. Immediately serve in a deep dish. Add bed of
sweet potato, corn, and lettuce.

# Ceviche Tostada

## Ingredients

1/2-3/4 lb. shrimp
2-3 firm tomatoes, diced in small pieces
1 medium red onion, diced in small pieces
1/3 cup cilantro
3 garlic cloves, minced finely
1 jalapeno, minced finely
2 tbsps. clam juice
2 limes, juice of
Salt
12 tostadas

## Directions

Place all ingredients except salt into a large plastic bag.
Vigorously shake bag to blend contents. Put bag in
refrigerator all night. In morning, remove excess liquid.
Add salt, and serve over Tostadas. Option: Cod and
halibut work well in this recipe. Option: Mix and match
shrimp with squid and octopus.

# Scallop Ceviche

## Ingredients

2-3 fresh scallops, very thinly sliced
1 dash fresh lime juice
1 dash lemon juice
2 red ripe tomatoes, chopped
1 green chile pepper, de-seeded and chopped
1 red chile, de-seeded and chopped
1 red onion, chopped

## Directions

Blend the scallops with the juice in a ceramic or glass bowl. Add the tomato, onion, and chilies to the bowl. Place lid on bowl, and put it in the refrigerator. Let marinate for at least 1 hour.

# Jalapeno Albacore Ceviche

## Ingredients

2 jalapenos, seeded and finely chopped
2 (6 oz.) cans albacore tuna in water, drained and broken up
1 bunch cilantro, chopped
1 large tomatillo, finely chopped
2 large firm tomatoes, chopped
2 lemons, juice of
1 dash sea salt
Corn tortilla chips

## Directions

Place all ingredients in a ceramic or glass bowl. Blend contents, and let mixture chill for 20 minutes. Serve Ceviche with tortilla chips.

# Scallops Ceviche

## Ingredients

3 1/2 lbs. small bay scallops
Lime juice
3 tbsps. orange juice
1 tsp. champagne vinegar
1/3 cup olive oil
1/8-1/4 tsp. Tabasco sauce, to taste
2 garlic cloves, minced
1 tbsp. fresh sweet basil, chopped, to taste
1 tbsp. fresh parsley, chopped, to taste
1 tsp. granulated sugar
Salt and freshly ground black pepper, to taste
2 medium red onions, finely chopped (sweet Italian onions)
1 (4 oz.) can mild green chilies, chopped (do not drain)
1 medium red bell pepper, chopped
1 medium yellow bell pepper, chopped
Grated orange rind, for garnish

## Directions

Place scallops in a bowl with lid. Add lime juice to bowl.
Seal bowl and refrigerate for 8 hours.
Next, remove excess liquid but do not rinse. Blend juice,
vinegar, oil, sauce, garlic, basil, parsley and sugar in a
separate bowl. Add salt and pepper as needed. Add all
remaining ingredients except for the rind. Vigorously
shake bowl. Taste and adjust seasoning as needed. Add

scallops and thoroughly mix. Refrigerate until serving. When serving, first re-mix to re-coat scallops. Next, place in lettuce-lined dish. Finally, place rind pieces atop contents.

**Note:** Flounder can be substituted for scallops.

**Note:** This recipe makes eight servings.

# Ceviche Salad

## Ingredients

1 lb. cooked sea bass; filet cut in 1/2 inch cubes or
cooked shrimp
3 limes, juice of
1 medium red onion, chopped
4 plum tomatoes, chopped
1 green pepper, seeded and chopped
4 tbsps. fresh cilantro, chopped
2 fresh garlic cloves, minced
Salt and pepper (optional)

## Directions

Place fish or shrimp in a bowl. Pour in the lime juice, and
mix. Add remaining ingredients, and re-mix.

Note: If using sea bass, then carefully stir to ensure the
fish remains intact. Refrigerate for at least 2 hours. Serve
cold.

# Mexican Ceviche

## Ingredients

13 lbs. tilapia fillets, uncooked, chopped
10 limes
10 lemons
3 medium purple onions, finely chopped
5 medium firm ripe tomatoes, finely chopped
2 sprigs fresh cilantro
2 (4 oz.) tequila
Salt and pepper

## Directions

Extract juice lemons and limes in a juice machine.
Combine fish and onions in a large bowl. Refrigerate for
at least 1 hour. Put remaining ingredients into bowl.
Refrigerator for at least 2 hours. Season with salt and
pepper as needed.

Note: More onions, tomatoes, and cilantro can be added
as needed.

# Ceviche Verde

## Ingredients

### CEVICHE

1 lb. fish fillet (mahi-mahi)
3/4 cup lime juice, freshly squeezed, strained
1 1/2 tsps. salt
1/2 tsp. dried oregano, crumbled

### SAUCE

1 cup fresh basil, lightly packed
1 cup flat leaf parsley, fresh, lightly packed
1/4 cup fresh cilantro leaves
15 fresh mint leaves
1 jalapeno, thinly sliced
1 garlic clove, sliced
1/2 tsp. sugar (or more to taste)

### TO SERVE

20 green olives, pitted and halved
1/2 white onion, small (about 2 oz.)
2 tbsps. olive oil
1 lime, juice of (as needed)
Salt, if needed (optional)
1 avocado, ripe, thinly sliced

## Directions

Place raw fish in a tall, narrow dish. Mix the juice, salt and oregano in a separate bowl. Pour entire contents of bowl onto fish. Refrigerate mix for at least 1 hour. In another bowl, add mix all remaining ingredients together. Add them to 1 cup of water, and place mixture in a blender. Blend until a smooth sauce is created. Taste, and add more sugar as needed. Remove excess liquid from fish. Place fish in a mixing bowl. Combine the sauce and the fish. Mix in olives, onion, oil and lime juice, and thoroughly blend. Taste, and add more salt or more juice as needed. Let mixture sit for 1/2 hour. Place Ceviche in individual serving bowls. Top with avocado slices as a garnish. Serve Ceviche with tortilla chips.

# Classic Ceviche

## Ingredients

1 lb. fresh skinless red snapper fillet, bass fillet, halibut
fillet or other ocean fish fillet, cut into ½" cubes
1 1/2 cups fresh lime juice
1 medium white onion, chopped into ½" pieces
2 medium tomatoes or 2 large tomatoes, chopped into
½" pieces (about 1 lb.)
1-3 fresh hot green chile peppers, stemmed, seeded and
finely chopped (2 - 3 Serrano's or 1 - 2 jalapenos)
1/3 cup cilantro, chopped, plus a few leaves for garnish
1/3 cup pitted green olives, chopped
1-2 tbsp. extra-virgin olive oil (optional)
Salt
3 tbsps. fresh orange juice or 1/2 tsp. sugar
2 small avocados, peeled, pitted and diced
Tostadas, tortilla chips, or saltine crackers for serving

## Directions

Combine fish, juice and onion in a bowl. Cover and
refrigerate for at least 4 hours. Drain without rinsing. Mix
the tomatoes, chilies, cilantro, olives and [optional] oil.
Add the fish and season with salt as needed. Pour in the
orange juice or add sugar. Cover and refrigerate. Before
serving, gently stir in the diced avocado.

Note: The fish may be marinated a day in advance after
sitting for about 4 hours.

Note: When the fish is cooked, drain it so that it will not become too tangy.

Note: For the freshest flavor, add the seasonings to the fish 2 hours in advance.

# Scallop Ceviche

## Ingredients

2 lbs. bay scallops, halved if large
3/4 cup fresh lemon juice
3/4 cup fresh lime juice
1/2 cup red onion, slivered
1/2 cup yellow bell pepper, slivered
1 cup pimento stuffed olive, halved (or sliced if large)
2 tbsps. olive oil
1 tbsp. fresh cilantro, chopped
3 slices lime peel (about 2 x ¼")
1 tsp. salt
3 dashes hot red pepper sauce

## Directions

Place all ingredients in small, square baking dish. Thoroughly mix, and cover dish with plastic wrap. Refrigerate contents for at least 8 hours. Remove zest, transfer to serving dish. Serve Ceviche chilled.

# Shrimp Ceviche

## Ingredients

1 lb. cooked shrimp, tails and shell removed
4 large tomatoes, chopped
1 avocado, chopped
1 red onion, diced
1 bunch fresh cilantro, chopped
2 cups tomato juice
2 tbsps. catsup, if needed
1-2 jalapeno, seeds removed and minced
1 lime, juice of
1 tsp. Sazon Goya seasoning, approx.
Salt and pepper, to taste

## Directions

Cut shrimp into small pieces. Add all other ingredients, and mix. Thicken with catsup as needed.
Add Sazon as seasoning. Add salt and pepper as needed.
Cover with lid and refrigerate for several hours. Serve with tortilla or blue-corn chips).

# Lime Ceviche

## Ingredients

1/2 cup fresh lime juice
1 small chile pepper, seeded and diced (optional)
1 tbsp. extra-virgin olive oil
1 cup sea bass, skin removed and diced
1 cup perch, diced
1 cup scallops
1 cup octopus, cleaned and diced
1/2 Spanish onion, sliced finely
1 cucumber, cut into matchsticks
1/4 cup fresh mint leaves
1/4 cup coriander, finely diced
1/4 cup parsley, finely diced
1 avocado, peeled, pitted, and diced
1/4 red capsicum, sliced finely
Salt and pepper

## Directions

Mix all ingredients in a bowl. Place the fish into mixture.
Refrigerate for at least 30 minutes. Drain liquid without
rinsing fish. Serve with tortillas, crackers or bread.

# Best Cevic

## Ingredients

1 1/2 lbs. raw shrimp, peeled and clean
5 limes, juice of
2 tbsps. minced jalapenos, divided
1/4 cup minced red onion, divided
1/4 tsp. salt
1 cucumber, peeled, seeded, and diced
3 avocados, diced
2 tomatoes, seeded and diced
1 bunch fresh cilantro, chopped (about 1/4 cup)
Tortilla chips or lettuce leaf

## Directions

Using cold water, rinse shrimp [or other small pieces of seafood]. Dry shrimp. Place in bowl or bag. Add juice, 1 tbsp. jalapeno, 2 tbsp. red onion, and some salt. Mix well to entirely coat shrimp. Refrigerate for at least 1 hour. During refrigeration, shake contents to ensure absorption.
Remove from refrigerator when ready to serve. Add remaining jalapeno and red onion. Carefully add cucumber, avocado, tomato, and cilantro. Taste and add more salt as needed. Serve with tortillas, crackers or bread.

Option: Add cocktail sauce, and serve as a salad over leaves of lettuce.

# Mango Scallop Ceviche

## Ingredients

1 lb. sea scallops, quartered
5 limes, juice of (approx. 1/4 Cup or so if limes are not juicy enough, use bottled juice)
1/2 cup raspberry vinegar
1 tsp. kosher salt
1 tsp. black pepper
2 green bell peppers
2 yellow bell peppers
2 red bell peppers, seeded and diced
1 1/2 red onions, diced
2-3 mangoes, diced
6 plum tomatoes, seeded and diced
4 tbsps. fresh cilantro, chopped fine
Tortilla chips
Crackers

## Directions

Combine ingredients in a ceramic or glass mixing bowl. Add scallops, juice, vinegar, salt and pepper. Seal mixture and refrigerate overnight. Occasionally stir mixture during marinating. On the next day, add the peppers, onions, mangos, tomatoes and cilantro. Carefully mix until blended. Add seasoning of choice. Serve with tortillas, crackers or bread.

# Coconut Tuna Ceviche

## Ingredients

10 oz. coconut milk
2 tbsps. ginger, chopped
2 tbsps. horseradish, grated
3 fresh jalapeno peppers, seeded and minced
3 tbsps. fresh cilantro, chopped
1 lime, juice of
12 oz. sashimi-grade tuna, cubed into medium pieces
1 tomato, seeded and diced
1 small red onion, julienned
1 scallion, julienned

## Directions

Boil milk, ginger, and horseradish in a pot. Reduce heat
by one fourth, and let simmer. Strain and let cool.
Combine tuna, tomato, jalapeno, cilantro, juice and sauce
in a bowl. Taste and add salt and pepper as needed.
Transfer to a serving bowl. Garnish with onion and
scallion.

Note: To increase flavor, make this dish a day in advance.

# Shrimp Ceviche

## Ingredients

3/4 cup fresh orange juice
1/4 cup fresh lime juice
1/4 cup fresh lemon juice
1/4 cup catsup
2 tsps. garlic, minced
1 1/2 lbs. jumbo shrimp, peeled, deveined and halved
lengthwise
1 cup tomato, seeded and chopped
1/2 cup red onion, slivered
1/4 cup minced fresh cilantro
2 tbsps. jalapenos, seeded, minced
2 tbsps. olive oil
1 tsp. kosher salt
2 dashes hot sauce
2 tbsps. fresh lime juice
1/4 cup kosher salt
1 cup avocado, diced
4 slices limes

## Directions

Boil juices, catsup, and garlic in a pot. Add shrimp, and
reduce heat to low. Let simmer for 2 minutes. Drain
liquid into a bowl and set aside. Place shrimp on a plate.
Cover and refrigerate.
Prepare a bowl of ice water. Float the bowl of citrus
juices in the ice water. Mix until cooled. Add tomato,

onion, cilantro, jalapeño, oil, salt and sauce. Add shrimp
and thoroughly mix. Refrigerate for at least 15 minutes.
Occasionally stir during refrigeration. Prepare glasses for
serving. Dip glasses in lime juice and then into kosher
salt. Ladle 1/4 cup of diced avocado into each glass. Top
with 1 cup of shrimp mixture. Use lime slices as a
garnish. Serve with crusty bread.

# Thai Coconut Ceviche

## Ingredients

2 lbs. raw shrimp, peeled and cleaned
1 whole sweet white onion
2 fresh jalapenos or Serrano's
1 bunch cilantro
1 (6 oz.) can coconut milk
2 inches fresh ginger, peeled
1/2 tsp. salt
6 limes, juice of

## Directions

Cut shrimp into small pieces. Section ginger into ¼"
slices and grind in food processor. Dice the peppers.
Chop the onion and cilantro. Thoroughly mix all
ingredients. Let sit overnight.

# Simple Peruvian Ceviche

## Ingredients

2 lbs. tilapia fillets or other firm white fish fillets, cubed
8-10 garlic cloves, chopped
1 tsp. salt
1/2 tsp. black pepper
2 tsps. fresh cilantro, chopped
1 Habanero pepper, seeded and chopped
8-12 limes freshly squeezed and strained to remove pulp,
enough to cover fish
1 red onion, thinly sliced and rinsed

## Directions

Put all ingredients except red onion in a pot. Blend well
and place red onion atop mixture. Marinate in the
refrigerator for at least 2 hours. Re-mix and serve with
lettuce, corn, avocado or other cold vegetables.

Note: Use a juicer that only squeezes the juice out of the
limes.

Note: Don't use one that tears the membranes as this
causes a bitter taste.

# Ceviche De Corvina

## Ingredients

1 lb. boneless fish, preferably White Sea Bass (Corvina)
1 1/2 cups onions, minced
1 1/3 cups lemon juice, fresh
1/2 cup celery, diced
1/4 cup cilantro, shredded
Salt
1/2 hot pepper, minced (optional)

## Directions

Cut the fish into small pieces. Place fish in a glass bowl.
Add all the other ingredients covering the fish.
Thoroughly blend. Cover bowl with plastic. Place in the
refrigerator for 24 hours. Serve with tortillas, crackers or
bread.

# Summer Seafood Ceviche

## Ingredients

1/2 lb. shrimp, peeled and deveined
1/2 lb. squid, cleaned and sliced into rings
1/2 lb. scallops, quartered if large
1 (10 oz.) can tomatoes
2 medium ripe tomatoes, seeded and diced
1/2 large cucumber, peeled and diced
1/2 large green pepper, diced
1/2 medium red sweet onion, finely diced
1/2 cup fresh cilantro, chopped
1 tsp. garlic, minced
3/4 cup lime juice
1/2 tsp. cumin
1 tbsp. capers, chopped
1/2 cup hot and spicy hot V8
1 tbsp. extra-virgin olive oil
1 tsp. Accent seasoning (optional)
Salt and pepper

## Directions

Fill a large pot with boiling water. Fill a large bowl with freezing water. Add shrimp to boiling water, and cook until pink. Plunge shrimp into cold water to stop the cooking process. Add squid to boiling water, and count to five. Plunge squid into cold water. Add scallops to boiling water, and cook for a minute. Plunge scallops into cold water. Separate seafood from liquid. Place it in a ceramic or glass bowl. Cover seafood with lime juice. Refrigerate mixture for 60 minutes. Separate tomatoes from their juice. Blend tomatoes and all other ingredients in a bowl. Place seafood, juice and seasoning into the mixture. Refrigerate for at least 180 minutes.

# Marinated Ceviche

## Ingredients

1 lb. white fish fillet (or a mixture of white and shell fish)
3-4 limes, juice of or lemons, juice of
1 red onion, thinly sliced
1 large tomato, peeled, seeded, and chopped
Green chile pepper, chopped
2 tbsps. fresh coriander or parsley
1/4 cup corn or olive oil
1 dash Tabasco sauce
1 tsp. Worcestershire sauce
1 small lettuce, shredded
1 ear corn, cooked, cooled and cut into 4 pieces

## Directions

Remove skin and rinse fish. Cut fish into small pieces.
Place fish in a glass bowl. Pour juice over fish until it is
completely covered. Add onion, tomato, chile and
coriander to the fish. Thoroughly blend. Seal bowl with
plastic. Refrigerate for at least 8 hours. Occasionally stir
mixture during refrigeration. Drain the fish, saving the
juice for later. Make a vinaigrette dressing with the oil and
2 tbsp. of the remaining juice. Add the Tabasco and
Worcestershire sauces to the dressing. Pour dressing over
the fish and mix. Serve on individual plates using lettuce
as a bed for the fish. Place corn atop the fish as a garnish.

# Salmon Mango Ceviche

## Ingredients

1/2 lb. salmon, diced
3-4 Roma tomatoes
1 small white onion
1 mango (not too ripe)
1 bunch fresh cilantro
2-3 Serrano peppers
10 limes, juice of
Whole wheat crackers

## Directions

Place salmon in lime juice. Let mixture marinate for at least 8 hours. Chop and drain remaining ingredients. Remove excess liquid from salmon. Combine salmon with mixture. Serve on tortillas, crackers or bread.

# Coconut Shrimp Ceviche

## Ingredients

1 lemon, halved
1 head garlic, halved
3 bay leaves
8 peppercorns
Sea salt
1 1/2 lbs. large shrimp, peeled
2 cups coconut milk
1/2 cup lime juice, plus more
Lime juice, for drizzling (about 6 - 8 limes)
1 red onion, sliced thin
2 Serrano chilies, sliced thin
1/2 bunch cilantro leaf, freshly chopped, plus more for garnish
4 coconuts split in half
Rock salt or kosher salt, for serving (about 2 cups)
Extra-virgin olive oil, for drizzling

## Directions

Making the Ceviche: Heat a large pot of water. Add lemon, garlic, bay leaves and peppercorns. Taste and add salt as needed. When boiling, add the shrimp, and turn off the heat. Let shrimp simmer for 3 to 5 minutes. Transfer shrimp to a pan and refrigerate. When cooled, slice shrimp in half lengthwise. Put coconut milk, lime juice, onion, chilies and cilantro in a bowl. Season mixture with salt as needed. Add the cooled shrimp. Let mixture marinate in the refrigerator for 30 minutes.

Preparing the Coconuts: Tap coconuts in center with a hammer. Gradually turn coconuts while tapping.

Note: Coconuts will eventually split into halves. Drain coconuts and save both liquids and shells.

Serving the Ceviche: Place salt on a large platter. Stand coconuts in salt. Ladle Ceviche into shells. Sprinkle lime juice, olive oil and cilantro onto shells as a garnish.

# Best Ever Ceviche

## Ingredients

1 lb. shrimp, cooked peeled, and chopped to bite size pieces
1 cup fresh lime juice, squeezed
3 cups fresh tomatoes, finely diced
1 diced green sweet pepper
1 1/2 cups fresh cilantro, chopped
1 tsp. salt
4 diced jalapeno peppers (take the seeds out if you like it mild, and leave them in for HOT)
1 tbsp. white vinegar
1 large onion, finely chopped
1 green onion, chopped
1/2 lb. imitation crabmeat, chopped

## Directions

Place all ingredients in a large bowl. Thoroughly mix. Let mixture sit in refrigerator for a few hours. Serve cold either on tostada shells, as a dip with chips, or in a dish to eat alone.

Option: Use lettuce, avocado, and black olive as a garnish.

# Ceviche De Gringo

## Ingredients

Seafood
1/2 lb. bay scallop or sea scallops (if sea 1/4 them)
1/2 lb. shrimp, uncooked
1 lb. firm white fish fillet
Aromatics and spices
1/2 bunch cilantro, if you're not sure add less then add
more if needed
1 red onion, washed with lime and 1 tsp. salt soak 10 min.
then rinse juice
2-3 Serrano peppers or jalapenos, seeded or 1 Habanero
pepper, seeded
1-2 tomatoes
1-2 celery ribs
1-2 garlic cloves
8-10 limes, juice of (squeeze all the juice)
3 tbsps. olive oil
Salt and pepper
Avocado
1/2 cup corn, off the cob
1/2 lb. octopus, cooked
1/2 lb. squid, uncooked

## Directions

Cut all seafood into ¼" pieces. Mince celery, onion,
peppers, garlic, tomato and cilantro. Place all ingredients
except the lime juice in a casserole dish. Entirely cover

mixture with lime juice. Seal and place mixture in the refrigerator. Let marinate for 2 hours. Serve with chips, crackers or bread.

# Ceviche Roll-Ups

## Ingredients

1 lb. firm white fish fillet, thawed and cut into bite-sized
pieces (such as cod, scrod, haddock)
2/3 cup fresh lime juice
12 oz. Jarlsberg cheese or reduced-fat Jarlsberg cheese,
shredded (reserve one cup for topping)
2 limes, zest of
1 medium tomato, seeded and chopped
2 green onions, chopped
4 oz. chile peppers, finely chopped, drained
1/2 cup fresh cilantro leaves, chopped
1 tsp. ground cumin
4 large radishes, sliced
12 oil-cured olives, seeded and chopped (optional) or 1/4
cup olive, pimento stuffed (optional)
8 flour tortillas

## Directions

Place fish in lime juice for 1 1/2 hours. Frequently stir
mixture as it marinates. Drain excess liquid leaving fish
moist. Place remaining ingredients except tortillas and
reserved cheese into a bowl. Warm oven to 375 °F. Place
1 cup of mixture on each tortilla. Roll each tortilla, and
place it in pan sprayed with nonstick oil. Place reserved
cheese atop each roll. Cover pan with foil, and bake for
25 minutes. Uncover mixture and cook for an additional
5 minutes. Serve as a main dish with black beans and

brown rice.

Option: Serve alone as an appetizer.

Option: Use vegetables with hot peppers, celery or diced jicama as a substitute.

Option: Use scallops as a substitute.

# Ceviche Mexicana

## Ingredients

1/2 cup fresh lime juice
2 tbsps. fresh lime juice
1 lb. shrimp (ideally 41/50 count to a lb.)
1/2 cup white onion, chopped into ¼" pieces
1/3 cup fresh cilantro, chopped, plus several sprigs for garnish
1/4 cup tomato, diced
1/4 cup catsup
1 tbsp. vinegary Mexican bottled hot sauce
2 tbsps. olive oil, preferably extra-virgin
1 cup cucumber or jicama, diced peeled (or 1/2 cup of each)
1 small ripe avocado, peeled, pitted and cubed
Salt
Tostadas or tortilla chips

## Directions

Boil 1 quart of salt water in a pot. Add 2 tbsps. of lime juice to pot. Drop in shrimp, cover pot and boil again. When boiling, remove pot from heat. Remove excess liquid, and save it for later. Replace the cover, and steam shrimp for 10 minutes. Let shrimp cool in a glass bowl. Peel and devein shrimp. Mix shrimp with the remaining lime juice. Cover bowl, and refrigerate contents for 1 hour. Rinse onion under cold water, and then dry. Add onion to shrimp mixture. Also add cilantro, catsup, sauce, [optional] oil, cucumber, jícama and avocado. Season with salt as needed. Cover and refrigerate. To serve, ladle the Ceviche into sundae glasses, martini glasses, or small bowls.

**Option:** Use cilantro leaves and lime slices as a garnish.

**Option:** Serve with tortilla chips.

# Sea Bass Ceviche

## Ingredients

1 lb. filet of fresh sea bass, cut into 1/2-inch cubes
1/2 cup lime juice, freshly squeezed
1/2 cup lemon juice, freshly squeezed
1/4 cup red onion, chopped
1/4 cup red bell pepper, minced
1/4 cup parsley, finely chopped
1/2 cup fresh cilantro, finely chopped
1/4 cup olive oil
1/2 tsp. sea salt, adjust to taste
1/4 tsp. ground pepper, adjust to taste
1/8 tsp. cayenne pepper (optional)

## Directions

Put fish in a mixing bowl. Add lime and lemon juices.
Cover, refrigerate and let sit for 1 hour. Add onions,
peppers, parsley and cilantro. Thoroughly mix. Cover,
refrigerate, and let sit for 2 hours. Add olive oil, salt and
pepper as needed. Serve on a bed of lettuce with crackers
on the side.

# Elena's Garbanzo Ceviche

## Ingredients

3 (15 1/2 oz.) cans garbanzo beans
1/3 cup cider vinegar
1 cup olive oil
1 onion, finely chopped
2-3 tbsps. fresh parsley, chopped
2 tsps. oregano leaves, dried
3 garlic cloves, finely minced
1 tbsp. catsup
1 1/2 cups chorizo sausages, chopped and fried (optional)
1 (6 oz.) can baby corn, drained and sliced (optional)
Salt
Cayenne pepper

## Directions

Combine all ingredients, and thoroughly mix. Place in refrigerator and chill for several hours. Serve with tortillas, crackers or bread.

# Party Shrimp Ceviche

## Ingredients

1 lb. small shrimp, without shells
3 tbsps. catsup
2 lemons, juice of, only
1 tbsp. Worcestershire sauce
2 tsps. soy sauce
1-2 tsp. hot pepper sauce (to taste)
1 red onion, thinly sliced
3 garlic cloves, crushed
1 sour dill pickle, diced
6 cherry tomatoes or grape tomatoes, halved
Salt and black pepper

## Directions

Cook the shrimp in boiling water for 5 minutes. Remove
excess liquid. Rinse shrimp in cool water. Place onions in
a colander. Pour boiling water over them, and let them
dry. Combine the catsup, juice, sauces, and garlic in pan.
Put shrimp and onions into a glass bowl. Pour the catsup-
lemon juice over the shrimp and mix. Add salt and
pepper as needed. Carefully add in pickles and tomatoes,
and mix. Refrigerate for at least 2 hours. Serve with
cocktail snacks.

# Barracuda Ceviche

## Ingredients

7 lbs. barracuda
4 large onions
3 large green peppers
6 hot peppers (plus seeds)
3 tbsps. salt
6 oz. apple cider vinegar
1 quart fresh lime juice

## Directions

Remove red meat from fish. Cut fish into ¼" cubes.
Place in large pan. Mince hot peppers, sweet peppers, and
onions. Place vegetables atop fish. Add vinegar and salt.
Add lime juice. Thoroughly stir for 5 minutes. Place
contents into a gallon jar and cover. Let mixture stand for
1 hour at room temperature. Refrigerate for 3 hours.

# Ceviche with Ahi Tuna

## Ingredients

20 oz. fresh Ahi tuna, cubed
1 fresh mango, peeled and cubed
1 fresh avocado, peeled and cubed
2 tbsps. red onions, minced
1 tomato, roasted, peeled and seeded
1 Serrano pepper, roasted, seeded and minced
1/2 cup fresh lime juice
1/2 cup fresh orange juice
1/8 cup tomato juice
1 dash Tabasco sauce
1 pinch sugar
Salt

## Directions

Note: Traditional recipes use catsup instead of tomato juice and sugar. Cut tuna into 1/4 inch cubes. Blend cubes with 50% of juices. Add all ingredients except the mango and avocado cubes.
Let mixture sit in refrigerator for at least 1 hour. Cut mango and avocado. Mix fruit with other 50% of juices. Put a small ring mold in the center of a serving plate. Ladle equal portions of mango, avocado, and Ahi into mold. Press down and remove mold. Promptly refrigerate contents.

Note: Make just before serving. Repeat for additional

portions. Surround mold with tortilla chips or corn nuts. Use chopped cilantro as a garnish.

**Option:** Place in a giant martini glass.

**Option:** Serve with chips on the side.

# Coconut Ahi Ceviche

## Ingredients

10 oz. coconut milk
1 tbsp. ginger, chopped
1 tbsp. horseradish, grated
12 oz. sashimi-grade Ahi, cubed into medium pieces
1 tomato, seeded and diced
Salt and pepper, to taste
1 small red onion, julienned
1 scallion, julienned

## Directions

Boil milk, ginger and horseradish. Reduce heat by one fourth and let simmer. Strain ginger and horseradish in fine sieve. Allow milk mixture to cool. Combine tuna and tomato with coconut sauce. Add salt and pepper as needed. Place Ceviche in individual serving bowls. Add onion and scallion as a garnish.

**Note:** This recipe makes four servings.

# Ceviche in Avocado Shells

## Ingredients

1 lb. trout, boned, skinned, and diced
1 cup lime juice
2 tbsps. olive oil
1 medium onion, chopped
1 (4 oz.) can green chilies, drained and chopped
1 medium tomato, peeled and chopped
Dried oregano
Salt
Pepper
3 ripe avocados

## Directions

Place fish in a ceramic or glass bowl. Add lime juice to bowl completely covering fish. Seal bowl, and refrigerate contents for at least 1 hour. Occasionally stir mixture during refrigeration.
Remove excess liquid leaving fish moist. Add next four ingredients, and thoroughly mix. Season with oregano, salt, and pepper as needed. Halve avocados lengthwise, and remove their seeds.
Remove avocado pulp [save for later] to create a deeper trough. Mince pulp, and place it in the fish mixture. Fill avocado troughs with fish mixture and serve.

# Shrimp Ceviche on Endive

## Ingredients

3 lbs. small raw shrimp, cleaned and minced
4 large tomatoes, seeded and minced
4 limes, juice of
3 lemons, juice of
1 cup cilantro leaf, chopped
1 Serrano chile pepper, seeded and minced
1/2 cucumber, peeled and minced
1 red onion, minced
Salt and pepper, to taste
3 tbsps. tomato sauce

## Directions

Place shrimp in a ceramic or glass bowl. Pour juice over the shrimp completely covering it. Refrigerate mixture for at least 1 hour. Add remaining ingredients to the mixture. Thoroughly mix until homogenous blend. Seal bowl and refrigerate it for additional 1 hour. Remove from refrigerator and uncover. Ladle spoonful of mixture onto end of an endive leaf. Arrange leaves on a platter as appetizer.

**Option:** Fill a martini glass with mixture and serve as appetizer.

# Shrimp Ceviche with Avocado

## Ingredients

3 lbs. medium shrimp, peeled and deveined
8 limes, juice of
8 lemons, juice of
2 oranges, juice of, preferably sour oranges
2 (14 1/2 oz.) cans petite cut canned tomatoes
1 red onion, cut into ½" cubes
1/2 bunch fresh cilantro, stemmed and roughly chopped
1 Serrano chili, roughly chopped
2 large avocados, peeled, seeded, and cut into ½" cubes
2 large cucumbers, peeled, seeded and cut into ½" cubes
1 medium yellow bell pepper, cut into ½" cubes (yellow)
1 medium red bell pepper, cut into ½" cubes (red)

## Directions

Clean and devein the shrimp. Cut shrimp into 1-inch pieces. Transfer shrimp to a glass bowl. Add fruit juice, and stir to combine. Refrigerate for at least 4 hours. Cut vegetables into small cubes. Place the tomato, onion, cilantro, peppers and chile into the shrimp mixture. Let mixture sit for 20 minutes. Carefully stir in the avocado and cucumber. Ladle mixture into eight chilled martini glasses. Place a few tortilla chips alongside the glasses.

Option: Remove avocado from recipe, but place slices of it on the side.

# Scallop and Snapper Ceviche

## Ingredients

4 oz. sea scallops, thinly sliced
4 oz. red snapper fillets, skinned and diced
1/2 cup fresh lime juice
1 large tomato, diced
1/2 medium avocado, pitted, peeled and diced
1 small red onion, minced
2 tbsps. fresh cilantro, chopped
2 tbsps. fresh lime juice
3 dashes hot pepper sauce
Salt
Ground pepper
Shredded iceberg lettuce

## Directions

Place scallops and snapper into a glass bowl. Add juice so
that it completely covers fish. Seal bowl, and refrigerate
for at least 1 hour. Remove excess liquid leaving seafood
moist. Add tomato, avocado, onion, cilantro; juice, sauce,
salt and pepper. Mix thoroughly, and refrigerate for at
least 1 hour. Serve cold on a bed of lettuce.

Note: Use sushi-grade fish to ensure flavor.

Note: This recipe is considered 5 points by Weight
Watchers.

# Crab and Avocado Ceviche

## Ingredients

1 lb. crab meat
2-3 Roma tomatoes, diced
2 medium avocados, cubed
1/2 cup fresh cilantro, chopped
1 garlic clove, chopped fine
5 green onions, sliced thinly
2 tbsps. fresh lemon juice
2 tbsps. fresh lime juice
1 tsp. chile powder
1 tsp. oregano
1/2 tsp. salt

## Directions

Cut seafood into cubes. Place all ingredients in a glass bowl. Thoroughly mix to create homogenous blend. Refrigerate for at least 2 hours. Serve with chips, crackers or bread.

# Scallop and Cucumber Ceviche

## Ingredients

1 lb. shrimp, cleaned
1/2 lb. cooked scallops
1/2 lb. white crab meat, cooked
4 lemons, juice of
4 limes, juice of
1 cup firm ripe tomatoes, diced
1 bunch cilantro, de-stemmed and finely chopped
2 avocados, diced
2 large cucumbers, peeled and diced
1/4 tsp. salt
1 tbsp. hot sauce

## Directions

Place shrimp in citrus juice until pink. Add scallops and crab meat to mix. Add cucumbers, tomatoes, avocados and cilantro to mix. Add salt and sauce to mix.

Option: Add a few diced Jalapeno peppers. Serve atop tostadas or with tortilla chips.

# Ginger and Soy Tuna Ceviche

## Ingredients

12 oz. high grade fresh ½" thick tuna steaks
3/4 bunch green onion, thinly sliced
1/4 small onion, finely diced
2 tsps. fresh ginger, grated
1/4 cup lemon juice
1/4 tsp. soy sauce
1/2 avocado, diced
1/2 mango, diced

## Directions

Place onions, green onions, ginger, jalapeno, juice, and sauce in a glass bowl. Thoroughly mix creating a homogenous blend. Cut tuna into ½" cubes. Place tuna in juice mixture so that it is completely covered. Seal bowl and refrigerate for at least 2 hours. Taste and add more juice or sauce as needed. Garnish with avocado and mango. Serve with rice crackers. tortilla chips or wonton wrappers.

**Option:** Serve in martini glasses.

# Halibut and Shrimp Ceviche

## Ingredients

1 lb. halibut
1 lb. shrimp
1 (6 oz.) container lump crab
Salt (to add to water to tenderize fish and or shrimp)
3/4 cup lime juice
1/4 cup lemon juice
1/2 tsp. salt
1 garlic clove, chopped
1-2 Aji Amarillo chile peppers, chopped (yellow Peruvian peppers)
1-2 jalapeno, chopped (to taste, remove seeds for milder spice)
1 tsp. parsley, chopped
1 tsp. cilantro, chopped
1/2 cup purple onion, chopped
3-4 lettuce leaves
4 ears corn, cooked and cut into 2-inch pieces
1 lb. sweet potato, roasted in the skin, peeled, and cut
1 lb. yucca root, peeled, cut, and boiled until soft

## Directions

Soften by soaking fish and shrimp in salt water for 1 hour. Remove excess liquid leaving fish and shrimp moist. Place all seafood in a ceramic or glass bowl. Add enough citrus juice to cover seafood. Add the salt, garlic, onion and peppers. Refrigerate for at least 20 minutes.

Add cilantro and parsley atop seafood. Separate seafood and liquid [save for later]. Line individual places with lettuce. Place the Ceviche in the center. Surround with corn pieces, sweet potato slices and yucca.

Option: Soak corn, sweet potatoes and yucca in saved liquid before using.

# Tuna Ceviche Lettuce Wraps

## Ingredients

250 g tuna fish cut in cubes
1 mango cut in cubes
1 avocado cut in cubes
For the sauce
4 tbsps. light soy sauce
4 tbsps. lime juice
Chile powder
2 tbsps. olive oil
2 tbsps. balsamic vinegar

## Directions

Place the tuna, avocado and mango in a glass bowl. Blend all the ingredients for the sauce. Combine the tuna and the sauce, and thoroughly mix. Serve with some Cevich lying on a bed of lettuce. Place remaining Cevich on the side for use with bread or crackers.

# Shrimp Ceviche with Oranges

## Ingredients

1 large tomato, halved, seeds removed
2 jalapeno peppers, halved, seeds removed
1 red bell pepper, halved, seeds removed
1/2 yellow onion, peeled
1 lb. medium shrimp, deveined, peeled, halved lengthwise
3/4 cup lime juice, freshly squeezed
1/2 cup orange juice, freshly squeezed
1/4 cup tomato juice
1 tbsp. sugar
1 1/2 tsps. kosher salt, plus more (or to taste)
Tabasco sauce
2 tbsps. chives, chopped
2 tbsps. scallions, finely sliced
1/4 cup cilantro, chopped

## Directions

Warm oven to 500 °F. Use foil to line a baking tray. Place peppers, onions and tomato on tray.

Note: Place these items cut-side down. Bake for 30 minutes until items are charred. Let cool by setting to side. Boil a large pot of lightly salted water. Add shrimp to boiling water, and turn burner off. Let shrimp simmer for 1 1/2 minutes. Remove shrimp from pot. Run freezing water over the shrimp. After it is chilled, place shrimp on paper toweling to dry. Place shrimp in glass bowl and set aside. Remove skins from peppers and tomato. Put skinned items and onion in a blender. Add the fruit juices, sugar and salt to the canister. Run blender until a smooth puree is evident. Season with Tabasco and salt as needed. Pour the blended sauce over the shrimp and thoroughly mix. Refrigerate combination until ready to serve. Garnish with chives, scallions, and cilantro. Serve in individual bowls.

# Flank Steak with Mushroom Ceviche

## Ingredients

3 lbs. flank steaks
6 oz. mixed baby greens
Mushroom Ceviche
2 lbs. button mushrooms
1/3 cup lemon juice, freshly squeezed
1/2 cup lime juice, freshly squeezed
1/3 cup orange juice, freshly squeezed
1/3 cup olive oil
1 red onion, thin sliced
1 red bell pepper, seeded, thin sliced
4 cloves garlic, minced
2 tbsps. fresh cilantro, chopped
Salt and pepper

## Directions

Add mushrooms, citrus juices and olive oil to a mixing bowl. Let mixture sit for 1 hour. Occasionally stir mixture. Add the onion, bell pepper, garlic, cilantro, salt and pepper to bowl.
Thoroughly mix, and then refrigerate for 2 hours. Grill the flank steak for 7 minutes on each side.

Note: This amount should produce a steak which is medium rare. Let steak sit for 5 minutes. Slice steak on the diagonal. Place mixed greens on plate. Place mushroom mixture atop greens. Then place steak slices atop mixture.

# Sopapillas with Fruit Ceviche

## Ingredients

Dough
1 (15 oz.) package Pillsbury pie crusts
Cinnamon, for sprinkling on dough
Honey, for drizzling
Vegetable oil, for frying
Fruit Ceviche
1/4 fresh pineapple
1/4 cantaloupe
1/2 pint strawberries
1/4 cup fresh orange juice
3 tbsps. tequila, flamed to remove alcohol
3 tbsps. honey

## Directions

Preparing the Ceviche: Dice fruit into similar-size pieces.
Mix orange juice and tequila with nectar, syrup or honey.
Refrigerate mixture for several hours. Serve as is or over
sopapillas with ice cream/sorbet/etc.

Making the Dough: Divided pie crust into four equal
sections. Fry crust until it is crispy, and remove it from
oil. Sprinkle with cinnamon or honey.

# Gourmet Shrimp Mojito Ceviche

## Ingredients

1/2 small red onion, finely chopped
2 garlic cloves, minced
1/4 cup fresh mint, chopped, plus about
30 leaves fresh mint, for garnish
1/2 cup fresh lime juice
Salt and freshly ground black pepper, to taste
2 lbs. shrimp, peeled and deveined with tail shells intact
(26 to 30 count)
30 slices French baguettes (1/2" thick)
1 1/2 tbsps. extra-virgin olive oil

## Directions

Put onions, half the minced garlic, mint, juice, salt and
pepper in a bowl. Add the shrimp to the bowl, and
thoroughly mix. Seal the mixture, and refrigerate it for 12
hours. During marinating, occasionally stir mixture to
coat shrimp. Rub the remaining garlic on the bread slices.
Place bread on a baking sheet. Warm oven to 350 °F, and
bake bread for 15 minutes. Place each shrimp on a bread
slice with its tail pointing up. Sprinkle shrimp and bread
with olive oil. Use the fresh mint leaves as a garnish.

# Lime and Chipotle Scallop Ceviche

## Ingredients

1 lb. sea scallops or bay scallop
1 tsp. olive oil
1/2 cup shallot, minced
1/2 tsp. chipotle chile in adobo, minced, or red pepper flakes, crushed
1/2 cup fresh lime juice
1/2 cup distilled white vinegar
1/2 cup water
8 oz. jicama, peeled and cut into ¼" matchsticks
1/3 cup cilantro, chopped
Lime wedge (for garnish)

## Directions

Wash scallops, and remove excess liquid leaving seafood moist.

Note: Halve large scallops with crosswise cuts making them 1/2" pieces. Combine oil, shallots and chilies in a pan. Fry for 3 minutes making shallots soft. Add lime juice, vinegar, and water to the pan. Boil mixture, and then simmer. Add scallops in a single layer, and re-boil. Cover and simmer for 2 minutes making scallops opaque. Remove scallops only, and place them in a glass bowl. Return mixture to a boil until it is reduced to 1 cup. Turn off burner, and add mixture to bowl completely covering scallops. Place lid on bowl, and refrigerate for at least 1 1/2 hours. Cut jicama into matchstick-sized pieces. Combine jicama and scallops. Ladle into individual-serving bowls. Add cilantro leaves and lime wedges as a garnish.

# Flounder Ceviche

## Ingredients

2/3 cup lime juice
1/2 tsp. sea salt
1 lb. sole or flounder
1 pinch pepper

## Directions

Toss all ingredients except fish in a glass bowl. Cut fish into 2 x ¼" strips. Place strips in juice completely covering them. Chill in refrigerator for at least 3 hours. Note: The lime juice "cooks" the fish making it safe to eat.

Note: If refrigerated, this recipe keeps for days.

# Shrimp and Coriander Ceviche

## Ingredients

3 lbs. small shrimp
1 bunch fresh coriander
2 red onions
1 jalapeno pepper
10 lemons, juice of
2 tbsps. olive oil
4 tbsps. tomato sauce or catsup
1/2 cup Worcestershire sauce
1 pinch salt

## Directions

Place shrimp, sauce, water and salt in a pan with oil and
fry. Remove excess liquid. Mince coriander and slice
onions. Put shrimp, coriander, onions and juice in a bowl.
Add jalapeno pepper, tomato sauce [or catsup] and olive
oil to bowl. Thoroughly mix. Taste and add salt as
needed. Place mixture in refrigerator for several hours.

# Ceviche Shrimp with Avocado Tacos

## Ingredients

3 limes
1 cup tomato, seeded and chopped
1 cup avocado, diced and peeled
1/2 cup cilantro, chopped
3/4 tsp. salt
1/4 tsp. black pepper
1 lb. cooked shrimp, peeled med. in size
1 jalapeno, chopped very fine (my own addition)
1 garlic clove, chopped very fine (another addition that I added)
12 corn tortillas

## Directions

Grate rind making 1 tbsp. Juice limes making 1/4 cup. Combine rind and juice in a glass bowl. Add all remaining ingredients.

[Option: Add finely chopped jalapeno pepper.]
Thoroughly mix and place lid on mixture. Refrigerate for 15 minutes. Occasionally stir during refrigeration.
Warm tortillas on a grill sprayed with oil.

# Ecuadorian Ceviche

## Ingredients

1/2 cup fresh lime juice
2 tbsps. fresh lime juice
1 lb. shrimp, unpeeled
1/2 medium white onion
1/3 cup fresh cilantro, chopped
1/2 cup catsup
1-2 tbsp. bottled hot sauce
2 tbsps. extra-virgin olive oil
1 cup cucumber, diced
1/2 cup tomato, diced
1 small avocado
Salt and pepper
1 large garlic clove
3 cups popped popcorn

## Directions

Boil 1 quart of salted water in a pot with a lid. Add 2 tbsps. of lime juice add shrimp and cover pot. Return to pot to a boil, remove from burner and loosen lid. Drain liquid [saving for later], replace cover, and steam shrimp for 10 minutes. Cool shrimp by spreading them out on a pan. When cool, devein shrimp. Add shrimp to remaining lime juice, and thoroughly mix. Refrigerate for at least 1 hour. Mince onion, avocado, cucumber, cilantro, garlic and tomato. Add these items to shrimp bowl. Mix items with catsup, hot sauce, and olive oil. Immediately serve, or cover and place in refrigerator. For a dramatic presentation, serve in oversized martini glasses.

Option: Add unsalted popcorn on top, and place popcorn along the sides.

Option: Add lime slices and cilantro leaves as a garnish.

# Scallop Ceviche with Avocado Dressing

## Ingredients

**Scallop Ceviche:**
1/4 cup fresh lemon juice, plus
2 tbsps. fresh lemon juice
3 tbsps. fresh orange juice
3 tbsps. fresh lime juice
2 tsps. lime zest, grated
2 tsps. fresh ginger, grated
2 tsps. Serrano chilies, minced
1 1/4 lbs. large scallops, sliced horizontally ¼" thick
4 scallions, finely chopped
1 red bell pepper, finely diced
1/4 cup cilantro, finely chopped
3 tbsps. pure olive oil
1 large garlic clove, minced

**Avocado Dressing:**
1 avocado, finely diced
1 small tomato (peeled, seeded and finely diced)
1 tbsp. red onion, minced
1 tbsp. cilantro, finely chopped
1 Serrano chili, seeded and minced (optional)
1 small garlic clove, minced
1 1/2 tbsps. fresh lime juice
1 1/2 tbsps. extra-virgin olive oil
Salt and freshly ground black pepper

# Directions

Preparing the Ceviche: Combine citrus juices with lime zest, ginger and chile in a glass bowl. Add scallops by placing them in a single layer. Ensure that the scallops are completed coated. Cover dish, and refrigerate it for 1 hour making scallops white. Add scallions, peppers, cilantro, garlic and olive oil. Refrigerate for at least 1 hour.

Making the Dressing: Combine avocado, tomato, onion, cilantro, chile and garlic in a glass bowl. Add the lime juice and olive oil, and the salt and pepper as needed. Divide the scallops, scallions and peppers among six shallow plates. Ladle the dressing onto the Ceviche. Place a bit of the marinade everywhere.

# Cheap Ceviche

## Ingredients

1 (6 oz.) can solid white tuna packed in water (drained)
1/2 cup lime juice (you can use a bottle or the juice of
about 5 key limes)
1 small tomato
1/4 large white onion
1/4 small red onion
1/2 jalapeno pepper

## Directions

Remove excess liquid from tuna. Flake tuna, and put it
into a glass bowl. Add enough lime juice to cover tuna.
Occasionally stir mixture. Chop the onions, tomatoes,
and jalapeno. Add these items to the mixture and stir.

Option: Leave the jalapeno seeds in mixture. Let mixture
marinate for 10 minutes. Occasionally stir mixture.

# Citrus Ceviche

## Ingredients

1/2 lb. medium shrimp, peeled and deveined and cut into
1/2 inch pieces
1/2 lb. bay scallop (the little ones)
2 lemons, juice of
2 limes, juice of
2 oranges, juice of
1 cup cucumber, peeled and diced into 1/4-inch pieces
1/4 cup red onion, finely chopped
1 cup tomato, diced
1 avocado, peeled, seeded, and chopped into 1/2-inch
pieces
1 tbsp. cilantro leaf, roughly chopped
2 tbsps. extra-virgin olive oil

## Directions

Place citrus juices in a glass bowl, and mix. Add shrimp,
scallops, cucumber and onions, and mix.

Option: Add chilies or peppers now as well, and mix.
Refrigerate for 3 hours until white.
Add tomato, avocado, cilantro, and olive oil, and mix.
Serve in martini glasses with saltine crackers on the side.

# Shrimp and Scallop Ceviche

## Ingredients

1/2 lb. shrimp, raw, peeled and deveined
1/2 lb. bay scallop, raw
3/4 cup lime juice (should completely cover shrimp and scallops)
1/4 cup tequila
1/4 cup lime juice (in addition to above lime juice)
1/4 cup tequila (in addition to above tequila)
1 large fresh tomato, seeded and diced
1 large cucumber, peeled, seeded and diced
1 cup fresh cilantro, pack loosely in cup, chopped
1/2 tsp. salt (more to taste)
1/4 tsp. white pepper
1/2 tsp. oregano
2 jalapeno peppers, seeded and chopped (wear plastic gloves to handle jalapenos!)
1 (3 7/8 oz.) can black olives, sliced
1/8 tsp. Tabasco sauce (or to taste)
1 avocado, peeled and sliced (optional)
8 oz. tortilla chips

## Directions

Cut shrimp and scallops into small pieces. Place seafood in bowl, and cover with lime juice. Add the tequila, and thoroughly mix. Seal bowl, and refrigerate overnight. Process all vegetables, herbs and spices except the avocado.

Note: Cut items into pieces smaller than the seafood.

Add vegetables to lime juice and tequila mixture. Add Tabasco sauce, and thoroughly mix. Seal bowl, refrigerate overnight. Remove excess liquid from the seafood. Combine the seafood with the vegetables. Thoroughly mix, and store in refrigerator. Serve with guacamole or avocado as a garnish. Add additional Tabasco sauce on the side. Eat with tortilla chips, crackers, or bread.

# Island Ceviche Salad with Pink Pickled Onions

## Ingredients

Pink Pickled Onions
8 oz. champagne vinegar
1/2 cup sugar
2 Serrano chilies, seeded
2 medium red onions, thinly sliced
Ceviche Salad
6 oz. fresh lime juice
1/2 lb. firm white flesh fish
1/2 lb. small scallop
1 medium solo papaya, peeled seeded and diced (save skins of 2)
2 plum tomatoes, seeded and diced
4 Serrano peppers, seeded and diced
1 cup Vidalia onion, finely diced
1/2 cup cilantro, chopped
1 jalapeno chile, seeded and diced
1 tbsp. white wine Worcestershire sauce
1 tbsp. Mexican hot sauce
2 oz. tomato juice

## Directions

Pickling Onions: Boil vinegar, sugar, and chilies in a pot. Stir mixture until sugar is dissolved. Put onions in a plastic container. Pour the hot mixture over them. Process container in an ice bath. Serve mixture chilled.

Making Ceviche: Put scallops and fish in lime juice. Thoroughly mix. Marinate overnight in refrigerator. Separate lime juice and seafood. Put seafood in a glass bowl. Add papaya, tomatoes, peppers, cilantro, and jalapeño to bowl. Add Worcestershire, hot sauce, and tomato juice to bowl. Thoroughly mix. Spoon mixture into papaya skins. Place pickled onions atop mixture as a garnish.

# Shrimp and Crab Ceviche on Fried Tortillas

## Ingredients

Canola oil
18 (5 inch) tortillas
1 1/2 lbs. medium cooked shrimp, peeled, deveined and chopped
3/4 lb. lump crabmeat
1/4 cup fresh lemon juice
2 tbsps. cilantro, chopped
1 large cucumber, peeled, seeded and chopped
2 large tomatoes, chopped
1-2 jalapeno chile, stemmed, seeded and finely chopped
1 small red onion, finely chopped
Salt
2 avocados, peeled, seeded and cut into slices
2 limes cut into wedges

## Directions

Place oil into a 1 inch deep pot. Warm pot to 350 °F. Fry each tortilla for 30 seconds, turning once. Place tostadas on a paper plate, and let cool. Add all ingredients except tostadas, avocados, and limes to a glass bowl. Salt to taste, and stir to combine. Place scoops of Ceviche on tostadas. Use avocado slices and lime wedges as a garnish.

# Filipino Ceviche

## Ingredients

1 kg skinned fresh sea bass, cubed to bite size pieces
2 tbsps. finely minced garlic
1 cup white vinegar
6 tbsps. lime juice
5 diced tomatoes
1 cup onion, finely minced
3 tbsps. gingerroot, finely minced
1 red bell pepper, diced
1 green bell pepper, diced
Jalapeno peppers
1/4 cup spring onion, minced
Salt and pepper

## Directions

Place fish in vinegar for at least 30 minutes. Chill in refrigerator. Remove excess liquid. Mix with lemon juice. Add all other ingredients. Thoroughly mix, and serve chilled.

# Tropical Scallop and Mango Ceviche

## Ingredients

1 lb. sea scallops, trimmed and sliced into 1/3" thick rounds
1 small red onion, thinly sliced
1/2 cup fresh lime juice (3 to 4 limes)
1/2 cup fresh orange juice (1 to 2 oranges)
1 tbsp. chives, chopped
Sea salt, to taste
Ground pepper, to taste
1 ripe mango, peeled, diced
1/2 cup avocado, diced
Romaine leaf (optional)
Orange slices (optional)
Lime slice (optional)
Star fruit, slices (optional)

## Directions

Bring large pot of salt water to a boil. Blanch scallops for 1 minute. Transfer scallops to a glass dish. Add citrus juices, onions, chives, salt and pepper. Thoroughly mix, cover, and refrigerate. Leave in refrigerator for several hours, occasionally stirring. Add diced mango and avocado. Serve on lettuce leaves with fruit slices as a garnish.

# Lime chile Salmon (Ceviche)

## Ingredients

4 skinned salmon fillets
4 limes, juice of
2 red chilies (more if you like it hotter)
2 tbsps. fresh coriander or cilantro, chopped
1/4 tsp. ground cumin
2 garlic cloves, finely chopped
4 cm fresh ginger, grated

## Directions

Tear salmon into small pieces. Place in a glass mixing
bowl. Add juice, chili, coriander, cumin and garlic. Ensure
that juice covers fish, and mix. Add salt and pepper as
needed. Pinch ginger to sprinkle juice onto salmon.
Carefully and thoroughly mix. Seal bowl, and refrigerate
for at least 4 hours.

# Lime Juice Ceviche

## Ingredients

2 lbs. fish fillets (such as flounder, sole, or red snapper)
Salt, to taste
1 cup fresh lime juice (about 12 limes)
1/2 tsp. salt
1 small garlic clove, chopped very fine
1-2 fresh chile peppers, seeded and chopped fine
(preferably Aji Amarillo)
1 tsp. parsley, chopped
1 tsp. cilantro, chopped
1 medium onion, chopped fine (1/2 cup)
3-4 lettuce leaves
4 ears corn, cooked and cut into 2 inch pieces
1 lb. sweet potato, roasted in the skin, peeled, and sliced
into 1/2 inch thick rounds
1 lb. yucca root, peeled, cut into little-finger-sized slices,
and boiled until soft

## Directions

Cut fish into 1 ¼" x ¼" strips. Soak strips in salt water
for 1 hour. Remove excess liquid. Transfer fish to a glass
bowl. Carefully pour in the lime juice. Add salt, garlic,
and Aji, and mix. Seal bowl, and refrigerate for 15
minutes. Add parsley, cilantro, and onion, and mix. Place
Ceviche in the center of a lettuce bed. Surround with
corn pieces, sweet potato slices and yucca.
Use seaweed, such as yuyu, as a garnish.

# Canned Tuna Ceviche

## Ingredients

1 (6 oz.) can solid white tuna packed in water
1 fresh jalapeno chile, seeded and minced (more or less to taste)
1 small red onion, peeled and finely chopped
1 ripe tomato, diced
1 tbsp. fresh cilantro, chopped
Salt
Fleshly ground black pepper
1/4 cup fresh lime juice (1-2 limes)
2-3 tbsps. extra virgin olive oil
Lettuce
Fresh cilantro stem, for garnish

## Directions

Remove excess liquid from tuna. Flake tuna onto a serving plate. Sprinkle with chile and onion. Allow mixture to sit for a few minutes. Add tomato, cilantro, salt and pepper. Thoroughly mix.
Drip lime juice onto mixture. Drizzle oil onto mixture. Serve over lettuce bed. Use cilantro leaves as a garnish.

# Alaska Salmon Ceviche

## Ingredients

1 lb. skinless Alaska salmon, cut into ½" cubes or slightly smaller
2/3 cup freshly squeezed lime juice
2/3 cup freshly squeezed orange juice
1 medium red onion, chopped into ¼" pieces
1 large fresh poblano chile
2 large seedless oranges
2 tbsps. small capers, drained
1/3 cup fresh cilantro, chopped, plus
3-5 leaves cilantro, for garnish
Salt
2 cups frisee or baby mesclun
Thinly sliced toasted French bread or crackers, for serving

## Directions

Place salmon cubes into a glass bowl. Add citrus juices and onion to the bowl. Note: Add enough juice to cover the salmon. Seal bowl, and refrigerate for at least 2 hours. Remove most of the juice from the bowl. Roast the poblano on an open flame (5 minutes).

Option: Roast it on a baking sheet 4 inches below a hot broiler (10 minutes).

Note: Roasting is complete when the skin is blistered and

blackened. Cover with a towel, let it sit for 5 minutes. Remove skin, stem and pod from poblano. Tear it open, and rinse it removing stray seeds and skin. Cut into 1/4-inch pieces, and place pieces in a large bowl. Remove orange rind and white pith, and cut the membranes. Halve the resulting segments, and add them to the bowl. Add capers, cilantro and salmon with the remaining juice. Taste, season with salt as needed. Seal bowl, and refrigerate. Place the lettuce in eight separate bowls or glasses. Ladle the Ceviche onto the lettuce. Add a cilantro leaf to each container as a garnish. Serve with flavored crackers or toasted bread.

# Sweet and Sour Ceviche

## Ingredients

1 lb. very fresh red snapper fillet, skin removed, chopped
into ¼" dice
1 cup tomato, finely diced
1/2 cup white onion, finely diced
1/2 cup fresh lime juice
1/2 cup fresh orange juice
2 tbsps. fresh cilantro, chopped
1 tbsp. olive oil
1 tbsp. jalapeno, minced
1 tsp. lime zest, grated
1 tsp. orange zest, grated
Salt and freshly ground black pepper
Lettuce, cleaned
Homemade Tortilla Nests
12 (6 inch) corn tortillas
4 cups corn or vegetable oil
Salt, to taste

## Directions

Making the Ceviche: Place all ingredients in a glass bowl.
Thoroughly mix to ensure seafood is coated. Seal bowl,
and refrigerate contents for 1 hour. Add salt and pepper
to mixture as needed.
Put lettuce leaves on serving plates. Place the nests atop
the lettuce. Ladle the Ceviche into the nests and serve.

Making the Nests: Warm oil to 360 °F. Soften tortilla in the oil. Remove from the oil, and julienne tortillas. Place a few julienne tortillas in a 1-cup ladle. Place a smaller ladle atop of the tortillas. Immerse both ladles in the oil. Fry for 2 minutes making tortillas crisp. Transfer to a paper plate. Season with salt and Essence. Repeat process until all tortillas are fried. Place the Ceviche in the warm tortillas.

# Roma Tomato Ceviche

## Ingredients

4 roma tomatoes, seeded, chopped or 2 large tomatoes,
seeded, chopped
2 avocados, pitted, peeled, chopped
1/2 white onion, chopped
2 jalapenos, seeded, chopped into small pieces
1/2 cup cilantro, large stems removed, chopped
1 lime
Salt
1/2 lb. cooked shrimp, tail-off, shelled, deveined, cut into
approximately ½" size pieces

## Directions

Place all vegetables in a glass bowl. Squeeze limes
dripping juice into bowl. Thoroughly mix contents. Taste
mixture, and add salt as needed.

Option: Add thawed, chopped shrimp to mixture. Let sit
in refrigerator for several hours before serving.

# Sea Bass Ceviche with Avocado Melon Salsa

## Ingredients

12-16 oz. Chilean sea bass
1/2 cup lime juice
1/2 cup orange juice
1 small onion, sliced
1 garlic clove, minced
1/2 tsp. salt
2 tbsps. cilantro, chopped
2 tbsps. parsley, chopped
2 jalapeno peppers, minced
Bamboo skewers
1 small avocado, diced
1 cup cantaloupe, cut into small cubes
1/2 cup red onion, diced
1/3 cup fresh cilantro, chopped
4 tbsps. fresh lime juice
1 tsp. lime zest

## Directions

An hour before grilling, soak bamboo skewers in water.
Clean and oil the grill grates, warm grill to high. Cut fish
into1 1/2 inch cubes. Place next eight ingredients in a
plastic bag. Add fish to bag, remove air, and seal.
Refrigerate contents for not more than 30 minutes.
Carefully combine ingredients for the salsa in a bowl. Seal
bowl, and place contents in refrigerator. Place fish on

bamboo skewers. Grill skewers on high heat for 2-1/2 minutes on one side. Flip, and grill for 2-1/2 minutes on the other side.

Note: Sear outside of fish, but do not overcook it. Serve skewers with salsa on the side.

# Vegetarian Ceviche

## Ingredients

1 (14 oz.) can hearts of palm, cut in rings
2 large tomatoes, diced
1/2 small red onion, diced
1/2 bunch fresh cilantro, chopped
2 jalapenos, diced
2 limes, juice of
1 tbsp. olive oil
Salt
Pepper
Avocado
Cucumber
Green bell pepper

## Directions

Cut hearts of palm into circle shapes, and remove centers.
Prepare everything else, and thoroughly mix. Serve in
oversize martini or margarita glasses. Use cilantro leaves
and black pepper to garnish.

# Scallop Ceviche on Black Pasta Cakes

## Ingredients

### Ceviche
1/2 cup white onion, thinly sliced
1 cup fresh orange juice
1 cup fresh lime juice
1 fresh jalapeño chile, sliced, including seeds
2 tbsps. kosher salt
24 medium sea scallops (1 1/4 lb.), tough muscles removed from sides if necessary and scallops halved horizontally

### Cakes
6 oz. black (squid ink) angel's hair pasta
1 tsp. extra-virgin olive oil
About 1 cup olive or vegetable oil

### Salsa
1/2 cup white onion, minced
1/2 cup fresh cilantro, chopped
1/2 cup fresh tomatillos, finely chopped
1/2 cup tomato, finely chopped
1 tbsp. fresh jalapeño chile, minced, including seeds
1 tsp. kosher salt

## Directions

Making Ceviche: Place onion, juices, jalapeño and salt in a glass bowl. Simmer 4 quarts of salt water, and poach scallops. Occasionally stir scallops, and cook them for 1 minute. Remove excess water, and mix with marinade. Seal bowl, and refrigerate for 3 hours.

Making Cakes: Boil a pot of salt water, and cook pasta. Remove excess liquid, saving 1 cup for later. Run cold water over pasta to stop cooking process. Combine pasta and oil, and thoroughly mix. Warm oil in a pan using moderate heat. Create the cakes by melting pasta into a 1 tbsp. measure. Transfer melt onto oiled pan by inverting it. If necessary, flatten and form into cake shape. Make cakes four at a time until finished. Cook them until crisp (1 minute per side). Remove oil by placing them on paper plates. Season with salt as needed. Making Salsa: Soak onion in cold water for 20 minutes, then rinse and drain. Add onion, cilantro, tomatillos, tomato, jalapeño and salt to a bowl. Seal bowl, and refrigerate mixture until served.

Assembling Hors D'oeuvres: Take scallops from marinade, and place one atop each cake. Put salsa atop cakes, and immediately serve.

# Ceviche Cocktail

## Ingredients

1/2 cup plus 2 tbsps. fresh lime juice
1 generous lb. smallish shrimp, unpeeled
1/2 medium white onion, chopped into ¼" pieces
1/3 cup fresh cilantro, chopped, plus several sprigs for garnish
1/2 cup catsup
1 to 2 tbsps. vinegary Mexican bottled hot sauce
About 2 tbsps. olive oil, preferably extra-virgin (optional, but recommended to smooth out sharpness)
1 cup cucumber or jicama, diced, peeled (or 1/2 cup of each)
1 small ripe avocado, peeled, pitted and cubed
Salt
Several lime slices for garnish
Tostadas or tortilla chips, store-bought or homemade or saltine crackers for serving

## Directions

Marinating the Shrimp: Boil1 quart of salt water in a pot, and add 2 tbsps. of lime juice. Drop in shrimp, seal and let the water return to a boil. Remove from the heat, loosen the lid, and remove excess liquid. Replace cover and steam the shrimp for 10 minutes. Spread out the shrimp in a glass bowl, and let them completely cool. Peel, devein, and place the shrimp on a firm work surface. Make a shallow incision down the back and remove intestinal tract. Combine the shrimp with the remaining lime juice. Seal bowl, and refrigerate for about an hour.

Making the Flavorings: Rinse onion under cold running water, let it dry and add it to the shrimp bowl. Add cilantro, catsup, sauce, [optional] olive oil, cucumber, jícama and avocado. Taste and season with salt as needed. Seal bowl, and refrigerate until serving.

Serving the Ceviche: Ladle into sundae glasses, martini glasses, or small bowls. Use cilantro leaves and lime slices as a garnish. Serve with tortilla chips, saltine crackers, or tostadas.

# Scandinavian Ceviche

## Ingredients

1 grapefruit
1/2 avocado
4 oz. pre sliced gravlax (or smoked salmon)
2 tbsp. red onion, finely diced

## Directions

Remove peel from grapefruit exposing flesh. Carefully remove individual slices. Cut these slices into ½" pieces. Remove peel from onion, and dice into small pieces. Remove peel from avocado, and cut into ½" pieces. Cut the salmon slices into ½" pieces as well. Place remaining ingredients in a glass bowl, and seal. Place bowl in refrigerator and chill for several hours.

# Scallop, Shrimp, and Squid "Ceviche"

## Ingredients

1 cup fresh Seville orange juice (or 1/2 cup regular fresh orange juice plus 1/2 cup fresh lime juice)
1 tbsp. bottled Jay Amarillo chile Purée (often labeled "Crema")
1/4 cup red onion, finely chopped
1/2 lb. cleaned squid
1/2 lb. sea scallops, tough ligament removed and scallops halved horizontally
1/2 lb. large shrimp in shell (21 to 25 per lb.), peeled and deveined
1/4 cup cilantro, chopped
1 ½ tsps. salt

## Directions

Place juice, purée, onion and salt in a glass bowl. Thoroughly mix contents making a homogenous blend. Cut squid tentacles in half lengthwise. Now cut bodies crosswise into ¼" rings. Simmer a pot of water on a stovetop burner. Using water, poach scallops and shrimp. Occasionally stir, and cook for 1 minute. Add squid and continue cooking for 40 seconds.
Occasionally stir throughout cooking process. Drain, and add squid to marinade bowl. Marinate with bowl uncovered. Refrigerate for at least 3 hours. Remove, and add cilantro to mixture. Ladle seafood into shallow bowls with a slotted spoon. Place marinade over seafood, and serve chilled.

# Scallop Ceviche on the Grill

## Ingredients

1 1/2 lbs. large sea scallops (about 20), with tough
ligament removed
3 tbsps. extra-virgin olive oil
1 tsp. salt
1/2 tsp. black pepper
1 navel orange
2 tbsps. fresh lime juice
3/4 seedless cucumber, halved lengthwise, cored, and
thinly sliced (2 cups)
2 tbsps. shallot, thinly sliced
1 to 2 tsps. fresh jalapeño chile, finely chopped, including
seeds
1/4 cup fresh cilantro, chopped
Special equipment: Five skewers (if using wooden, soak
in water 30 minutes)

## Directions

Add scallops to 1 tbsp. oil, 1/2 tsp. salt and 1/4 tsp.
pepper. Place these items in a bowl, and thoroughly mix.
Then place four scallops on each skewer.

Prepare grill: Oil grill rack, and set grill on high. Grill
scallops, covered only if using a gas grill. Turn skewers
over once during cooking process. Grill for 5 minutes
until cooked through. Transfer skewers to a plate and let
them cool. Remove peel and pith from orange. Carefully
remove individual sections. Chop orange creating 1/4
cup of pieces. Transfer pieces to a large bowl. Add lime

juice, cucumber, shallot and jalapeño. Add remaining oil, salt and pepper to bowl. Halve scallops crosswise (quarter if large). Add scallops to cucumber mixture. Thoroughly mix to combine contents. Seal bowl, and let it marinate for at least 1 hour. Add cilantro just before serving.

# Shrimp Ceviche with Carrot, Orange, and Fennel

## Part One

### Ingredients

Oil:
1/2 cup canola oil
1/2 tsp. turmeric finely grated
1 tbsp. fresh lemon zest,
Sauce:
1 qt. fresh carrot juice (from about 3 1/2 lb. carrots)
1 qt. fresh orange juice
1 tbsp. fresh ginger, minced, peeled
2 stalks fresh lemongrass (lower 6" only), thinly sliced crosswise
2 fresh Thai red chilies, minced, including seeds
Salad:
2 lb. large shrimp in shell (21 to 25 per lb.), peeled and deveined
2 carrots cut into very thin matchsticks
3 navel oranges
1 fennel bulb, halved lengthwise
1 small red onion, halved lengthwise
3/4 cup fresh lime juice
1/4 cup 1" pieces fresh chives
2 tbsps. fresh mint, finely chopped
1/2 tsp. salt, or to taste

# Shrimp Ceviche with Carrot, Orange, and Fennel

Part Two

## Directions

Making Oil: Cook oil, turmeric and zest in a pan using low heat. Frequently stir, and cook for 5 minutes. Transfer to a smaller bowl, and refrigerate for at least 1 hour. Remove from refrigerator, and strain to discard solids. Making Sauce: Combine sauce ingredients in a pot. Boil, stirring occasionally, until reduced to 2 cups. Note: This process should take 30 to 40 minutes. Pour into bowl through strainer to discard solids. Place that bowl in a larger bowl of ice water. Note: This process will quickly chill sauce. Making Salad: Place shrimp into a pot of boiling salt water. Cook until cooked through (1 to 2 minutes). Drain, and transfer to a bowl of ice water. Drain, and halve shrimp lengthwise. Seal bowl, and refrigerate for several hours. Heat 4 tbsps. lemon oil in a pan. Sauté carrots in oil for about 3 minutes. Spread carrots across a serving plate. Refrigerate until chilled. Grate zest from oranges into a glass bowl. Remove remaining rind and white pith from oranges. Cut orange segments free from membranes. Add these segments to the zest. Cut fennel and onion crosswise. Add carrots to orange mixture. Also add fennel, onion, juice, remaining lemon oil, chives, mint and salt. Place Ceviche on eight plates and place shrimp atop mixture. Put 3 tbsps. of carrot sauce onto mixture.

# Shellfish and Watermelon Ceviche

## Ingredients

1 navel orange
1/2 cup plus 2 tbsps. fresh orange juice
1/4 cup fresh lime juice
1/2 cup (1/4") seeded watermelon, diced
1/2 tsp. fresh ginger, finely grated, peeled
1 1/2 tbsps. red onion, finely diced
2 to 3 tsps. fresh jalapeño chile, finely chopped
1/2 tsp. salt
1/4 lb. sea scallops, tough muscle removed from side of each if necessary and scallops cut into 1/2-inch pieces
1/4 lb. large shrimp in shell (21 to 25 per lb.), peeled, deveined, and cut into ½" pieces
1/4 lb. cooked lobster meat, cut into ½" pieces
1 1/2 tbsps. fresh mint, chopped
4 heads Bibb or 2 heads Boston lettuce (1 1/4 lb.)

## Directions

Remove peel and pith from orange. Cut segments free from membranes. Chop enough segments to measure 1/4 cup. Stir together orange, juice, watermelon, ginger, onion, jalapeño and salt. Place these items in a glass bowl. Boil 3/4 quart of water, and add scallops. Reduce heat to simmer, and poach scallops for 1 minute. Use slotted spoon to transfer scallops to a bowl of ice water to stop cooking. Boil again, and poach shrimp in a similar manner. Drain shrimp and transfer to bowl of ice water to stop cooking. Let scallops and shrimp dry. Add scallops, shrimp, lobster, and mint to watermelon mixture. Thoroughly mix and season with salt as needed. Seal bowl, and refrigerate for at least 1 hour. Trim and separate lettuce leaves for garnish. Serve Ceviche with lettuce leaves on the side.

# Mahi-Mahi Ceviche

## Ingredients

1 lb. mahi-mahi fillets cut lengthwise into 1/4-inch-thick strips
1 1/2 cups fresh lime juice
1 1/2 tsps. dried Mexican oregano
1/2 red onion, thinly sliced
4 jalapeño chilies, seeded; 2 minced, 2 thinly sliced
1/4 cup toasted unsweetened shredded coconut
3 tbsps. fresh cilantro, chopped
Saltine crackers

## Directions

Place fish, juice, and oregano in glass bowl. Sprinkle with salt, and thoroughly mix. Refrigerate until white (about 1 hour). Occasionally stir during refrigeration. Separate juice and fish, leaving it moist. Place fish back in mixing bowl. Add onion, jalapeños, coconut and cilantro. Thoroughly mix, and season with salt. Refrigerate for at least 20 minutes. Serve in oversize martini glasses. Place crackers on the side of glasses.

# Shrimp and Scallop Ceviche

## Ingredients

1/4 tsp. crumbled saffron
1 (8-oz) bottle clam juice
2 tbsps. red onion, diced
2 tbsps. seeded yellow tomato, diced
2 tbsps. scallions, chopped
2 tbsps. fresh chives, chopped
1 tbsp. fresh cilantro, chopped
3/4 to 1 tsp. Jay Amarillo
6 tbsps. fresh orange juice
1/4 cup fresh lime juice
2 bowls of ice water
1 lb. shrimp, shelled and deveined
1/2 lb. bay scallops (or quartered sea scallops)
A red and a green jalapeño chile, thinly sliced crosswise
for garnish

## Directions

Place saffron in a pan and heat on low. Toast saffron
until it is fragrant. Add clam juice to pan. Simmer mixture
until reduced to 1/2 cup (about 5 minutes). Set saffron
"broth" to side, and let it cool. Blend citrus juices,
Amarillo and saffron broth in a large bowl. Add
vegetables and herbs to bowl, and mix. Prepare two
bowls of ice water. Halve shrimp by cutting it lengthwise.
Remove tough muscles from scallops. Boil shrimp in 4
quarts of salt water. Occasionally stir until each shrimp is
cooked through (about 40 seconds). Remove shrimp with
a slotted spoon. Place shrimp in bowl of ice water.

Process scallops in a similar manner. Remove and discard excess liquid. Add seafood to saffron broth mixture. Add salt and hot pepper sauce as needed. Seal bowl, and refrigerate for at least 1 hour. Use jalapeño slices and a cilantro leaves as a garnish.

# Ceviche De Pescado

## Ingredients

2 lbs. white-fleshed skinless fish fillets such as flounder, sole, or cod
Salt
1 cup fresh lime juice (about 12 limes)
1/2 tsp. salt
1 small clove garlic, chopped very fine
1 or 2 fresh Aji Amarillo (yellow Peruvian chili), seeded and chopped fine, or substitute the canned Aji
1 tsp. parsley, chopped
1 tsp. cilantro, chopped
1 medium onion, chopped fine (1/2 cup)
3 or 4 lettuce leaves
4 ears of corn, cooked and cut into 2-inch pieces
1 lb. sweet potatoes, roasted in the skin, peeled, and sliced into 1/2-inch-thick rounds
1 lb. yucca, peeled, cut into little-finger-sized slices, and boiled until soft
A few strands of yuyu

## Directions
Cut the fish into 1 ½" x ¼" strips. Soak the strips in salt water for 1 hour. Drain salt water, and place fish into a glass bowl. Add the lime juice, completely covering the fish. Add the salt, garlic, and Aji. Refrigerate for 20 minutes. Remove and uncover. Add the parsley, cilantro, and onion. Create a bed of lettuce on a serving platter. Place the Ceviche in the center. Surround it with corn pieces, sweet potato slices and yucca. Use the optional seaweed as a garnish.

# Avocado Shrimp Ceviche

## Ingredients

2 lbs. large shrimp - peeled, deveined and chopped
3/4 cup fresh lime juice
5 roma (plum) tomatoes, diced
1 white onion, chopped
1/2 cup fresh cilantro, chopped
1 tbsp. Worcestershire sauce
1 tbsp. catsup
1 tsp. hot pepper sauce
Salt and pepper to taste
1 avocado - peeled, pitted and diced
2 (4 oz.) packets saltine crackers

## Directions

Put shrimp and lime juice in a glass bowl. Thoroughly stir
to ensure shrimp are completely coated. Let mixture sit
for 5 minutes. Add tomatoes, onion, and cilantro until
they too are coated with lime juice. Seal bowl, and
refrigerate for at least 1 hour. Remove shrimp from
refrigerator, and uncover bowl. Add Worcestershire
sauce, catsup, hot sauce, salt and pepper. Place avocado
pieces atop mixture. Ladle into glass tumblers. Set out
extra Worcestershire sauce, catsup, and lime wedges.
Serve with saltine crackers, tortilla chips, or bread.

# Pico de Gallo Ceviche

## Ingredients

1 (6 oz.) fillet orange roughly, or another firm white fish
fillet
15 limes, juiced
1/2 lb. cooked shrimp (optional)
2 tbsps. cilantro, chopped
5 green onions, chopped
1 red onion, diced
2 avocados - peeled, pitted, and chopped
2 fresh tomatoes, chopped
2 celery ribs, chopped
Pico de Gallo
2 tsps. salt
1 pinch black pepper

## Directions

Cut the raw fish into cubes. Spread across bottom of a
glass dish. Add enough lime juice to completely cover the
fish. Seal bowl, and refrigerate for 24 hours. Remove fish
from the refrigerator, and uncover bowl. Mix in shrimp,
cilantro, onions, onions, avocados, tomatoes and celery.
Add Pico de Gallo. Add salt and pepper. Cover, and
refrigerate for 12 hours. Serve chilled.

# Mexican Ceviche

## Ingredients

5 large lemons, juiced
1 lb. jumbo shrimp, peeled and deveined
1/4 cup fresh cilantro, chopped, or to taste
Tomato and clam juice cocktail
2 white onions, finely chopped
1 cucumber, peeled and finely chopped
1 large tomatoes, seeded and chopped
3 fresh jalapeno peppers, seeded and minced
1 bunch radishes, finely diced
2 cloves fresh garlic, minced
Tortilla chips

## Directions

Place either whole or chopped shrimp in a glass bowl.
Add lemon juice, completely covering shrimp. Seal bowl,
and refrigerate for 30 minutes. Remove bowl, and
uncover it. Place tomatoes, onions, cucumber, radishes
and garlic in bowl. Thoroughly mix contents. Add
cilantro and jalapenos slowly until desired taste is
obtained.

Note: Jalapenos will become stronger during marinating.
Add tomato and clam juices until desired consistency is
obtained. Seal bowl, and refrigerate for at least 1 hour.
Serve chilled with tortilla chips, crackers, or bread.

# Crawfish, Crab and Shrimp Ceviche

## Ingredients

1/2 lb. cleaned, cooked crawfish tail meat
1/2 lb. jumbo lump crabmeat
1/2 lb. cooked small shrimp, peeled and deveined
1/2 cup lime juice
1/2 cup catsup
2 tbsps. hot sauce
2 tbsps. olive oil
1/3 cup cilantro, chopped
1/2 cup red onion, diced (1/4" pieces)
1 cup cucumber, peeled, seeded, and diced
1 cup jicama, diced
1 jalapeno chile pepper, seeded and minced
Salt to taste
1 large avocado, diced

## Directions

Put all seafood in a glass bowl. Note: Carefully remove shells from meat. Add lime juice, and gently mix.

Note: Carefully mix; do not break up crab meat. Seal bowl, and refrigerate for at least 1 hour. Place catsup, hot sauce, and olive oil in another bowl. Add cilantro, onion, cucumber, jicama, and jalapeno. Taste, and add salt as needed. Carefully add this mixture to the seafood. Keep chilled until ready to serve. Use the avocado as a garnish.

# Citrus Ceviche

## Ingredients

1/2 cup fresh lemon juice
1/4 cup fresh lime juice
1/4 cup fresh orange juice
1 tsp. fresh ginger, grated
2 tbsps. extra virgin olive oil
1 lb. fresh sea bass fillets, sliced ¼" thick
1/4 cup fresh cilantro, chopped
1 onion, thinly sliced
2 avocados - peeled, pitted, and cubed
Salt and pepper to taste
4 hard-cooked eggs, quartered

## Directions

Combine the lemon juice, lime juice, ginger and olive oil in a glass bowl. Add the bass and completely mix to ensure it is coated. Seal bowl, and let it marinate in the refrigerator for 2 hours.

Note: Fish should turn white and be opaque when "cooked." Add the cilantro, onion and avocado to the bowl. Taste, and add salt and pepper as needed. Thoroughly mix, and serve with slices of hard-boiled egg.

**DISCLAIMER AND/OR LEGAL NOTICES:** Every effort has been made to accurately represent this book and it's potential. Results vary with every individual, and your results may or may not be different from those depicted. No promises, guarantees or warranties, whether stated or implied, have been made that you will produce any specific result from this book. Your efforts are individual and unique, and may vary from those shown. Your success depends on your efforts, background and motivation.

The material in this publication is provided for educational and informational purposes only and is not intended as medical advice. The information contained in this book should not be used to diagnose or treat any illness, metabolic disorder, disease or health problem. Always consult your physician or health care provider before beginning any nutrition or exercise program. Use of the programs, advice, and information contained in this book is at the sole choice and risk of the reader.

Made in the USA
San Bernardino, CA
08 July 2019